Cover Art:

Edison Goncalves

Edison Goncalves is a gifted illustrator whose art is enjoyed all over the world by young and old. Born in Brazil, he moved to Ireland and grew as an artist. His work with 20th Century Fox Animation Studios began his professional career and moved him to the United States. For 30 years he has shared his art and his creative vision with us all.

"For me, painting is a form of meditation, a way of switching off the part of my brain normally reserved for day-to-day issues and concerns."

ISBN: 978-0-9967754-0-3

If Only the Bears Had Left a Note

Parents already know how
to love their children into talking.
This book will help give those skills a ride
into the magical world of
writing and reading.

Parent

"I love this book! As a parent I can honestly say I wish I had this as a resource when my boys were younger. I would have worried less about their writing; enjoying what they were putting on paper knowing that, in time, all the spelling and grammar would be corrected. God bless the teachers who realize this already and embrace it in their classrooms!"

Teacher/Daughter

"A great reminder that the method of teaching reading and writing should always find its roots in a child's deep desire to express themselves."

Parent of a Kindergartner

"We have you to thank for inspiring our son and literally hundreds of other kids to get excited about reading and writing."

Daughter-In-Law

"Really inspiring reading I guess is what describes it best. Like I can't wait 'til tomorrow's scribblings and drawings and writings."

Son of the Author

"...it's hard to read through tears."

Dedicated and Overwhelmingly Thankful to:

Rich
For his patience and never ending love and support.

Micah, Karin, Alma & Leon
Jacob, Robin, Maeci & Gracelyn
Sarah & Chris, Jon & Leah
*For the grand experiences they all provided by
being part of the bizarreness of our family.*

John Clark
*The best principal a teacher or student could have the
privilege to know.*

Carole Edelsky
*For being my mentor for 30 years and reading this
manuscript more times than anyone should ever choose to
read anything.*

All the children and teachers
I had the privilege to work with over 37 years.
Especially the best preschool teacher ever, Gail, and
my early classroom mentor Diane Feldman Schoen.

If Only the Bears Had Left a Note

```
**************************************
*  *Two Ways to Read this Book*  *
*                                      *
*  Tucked within the text of the book are bordered  *
*  boxes like this one with personal examples of how  *
*  the surrounding ideas looked, personalized in my  *
*  classrooms or family. Ignore them, read them later  *
*  or read them with surrounding text.  *
*  You are in charge!  *
*  Don't say I didn't warn you.  *
**************************************
```

WHY A BOOK ABOUT WRITING?

"Adults teach children in three important ways: The first is by example, the second is by example, the third is by example."
Albert Schweitzer (Memoirs of Childhood and Youth)

This book has been rattling around in my brain for over 40 years. When I was younger, between being a single parent of three kids and teaching, I was too busy to tackle a book. Now I have grandchildren whose parents are bombarded with packaged reading programs and preschools that only use writing for food gluing exercises, one embarrassed letter at a time. Gluing popcorn on the letter "P" may make for tasty art and some children might remember what was under the coated snack they ate off the page later, but the only connection to reading and writing was probably creating an urge to eat in the presence of letters.

Writing, reading and talking are connected. They encourage one another. As they become part of a child's daily life they grow together. We all naturally go about our day talking and somehow our children learn the power and skills of speaking. Reading and writing need the same freedom and exposure we give to talking. Families that talk together can also read and write together. Just like Scout, who learned to read by being raised in a home surrounded by reading and writing in Harper Lee's To Kill a Mockingbird. My own children didn't remember learning to read or write...or talk.

This book is my attempt to help families create that same passion and just-like-breathing taken for granted-ness, not just for reading, but also for writing. Parents are surrounded by 'professionals' and the companies they represent, insisting that they need to isolate reading or writing in programs. I want families to understand and experience how to make both activities part of their daily lives. Parents and children should bask in the fun and memories of reading and writing together at home.

There are two main reasons you don't see a lot of books about writing with young children. First, not many people understand how writing works with young children. And second, those who do understand know that something as personal and creative as writing can be damaged by clipping its wings and trying to control and evaluate it. Instead of being a powerful friend, writing becomes a boring, judgmental pet. They are right that, in the wrong hands, explicitly teaching young children to write can be stifling instead of empowering. Most of the reading and writing programs that cram shelves everywhere parents shop are proof of that.

But parents are their children's most important resources. I believe that with a little background knowledge and a few ideas, parents can use writing as naturally with their children as they use talking. The first thing a parent, grandparent, or other significant adult in a child's life needs to do is to learn and abide by the writing code. Repeat after me, "I promise to relax, have fun, never worry or compare my child with other children and most of all, enjoy my child." So there you go!

Encouraging children to experiment with language seems to come naturally to parents when their babies are learning to talk. But, often, that stops when those same babies grow up a little and begin to write. Unlike talk, writing is there for all to see and evaluate. So instead of enjoying attempts, we have learned to fear mistakes. As a mother, grandmother and teacher, who talks to other mothers, grandmothers and teachers, I know that when people who care about young children really understand the connection between the processes of talking and writing, everyone benefits. Evaluation, fear and competition disappear in favor of celebration and awe.

Creating an environment that supports writing is an exciting and constantly changing process. If you need right and wrong answers and quick fixes, this book is probably not for you.

WHAT WE NEED TO KNOW ABOUT LEARNING TO WRITE

"When the first baby laughed for the first time, the laugh broke into a thousand pieces and they all went skipping about, and that was the beginning of fairies."
James Matthew Barrie (author of *Peter Pan*)

Helping kids learn to write is a lot like how you teach them to talk. The attitude is the same. So let's look at what you are already good at. Parents naturally talk to their babies about everything from evaluations of diaper contents to the joy of tasting (maybe not at the same time). Comments they make about baby noses and ears and games they play about piggy toes going 'wee wee wee' and little hands baking cakes 'as fast as they can' are sound tracks to daily life. These ongoing commentaries about baby life would make a sportscaster proud. Toe munching, tummy raspberries, 'oopsies' and comforting hums fill a baby's world with a feast for their listening pleasure. All this is accompanied by tickling, slobbering, hugging, rescuing and the other amazing sights and experiences of baby-dom.

Parents and grandparents use books and songs to continue swaddling their darlings in sounds of love. They reveal their theatrical side as they burst out with the best lion and mouse voices any toddler could ask for. They compose lullabies for sleep and folk songs about poopy pants, clean up or random events of the day. Babies are the perfect audience. They are spellbound by the virtuoso abilities of their talented mom or dad. Of course these interactions are not evaluated. They are enjoyed, recorded and shared. They become traditions, passed down through generations as grandparents love, amuse and indulge their tiny *dreams come true* in front of proud parents.

Babies also hear their own spontaneous reactions to life and every cry, coo, giggle or shriek is met by an adult response. These responses are generally positive or withheld for a purpose. For instance, parents might ignore whining or tantrum sounds while awaiting quieter moments for interaction. Moments where the decibel levels don't precipitate hearing loss. But when a toddler says, "Wah wah," for water, excited parents run for the sippy cup as they whip out their cell phone to record the history making verbiage that, of course, is not heard again for several days. But the story, now legend, appears on every social media site and is the main subject of dinner conversation.

No one rushes to correct the child by reciting 'T' and 'R' sounds. The little one begins to understand the power of the spoken word and listens to the voices of others in a different way. Through playing with sounds young children use their mouth as a tool to communicate. Their mouth is a very practical tool. Its uses are both purposeful. ("Up,") and powerful, ("No!") And parents respond to what their baby means. They don't evaluate how it is said. They just enjoy the fun of communicating with their child.

Parents already know how to love their children into talking. This book will help give those skills a ride into the magical world of writing. Actually, there is nothing magical about how it's done. But there is a lot of magic in the family stories and the confidence and skills kids gain in the process. The traditional view of teaching writing puts it at a desk in school or at the kitchen table at home under bright lights intended for food consumption. Don't limit yourself to one scenario. There are no writing police and you are the parent! This book will give you reasons and practical ideas to unchain writing from the kitchen table and make it a bigger part of normal family life. So 'MOVE AWAY FROM THE TABLE,' enjoy your family and write. No worries!

GROWING A WRITER: HOW DO YOU START?

"When we are writing, or painting, or composing, we are, during the time of creativity, freed from normal restrictions, and are opened to a wider world, where colors are brighter, sounds clearer, and people more wondrously complex than we normally realize."
Madeleine L'Engle (author of A Wrinkle in Time)

Writing happens a lot like playing with blocks. Imagine, the blocks are out and you and your child, start to play with them. As they chew on the plastic corners, you begin to build. Over time you play side-by-side, building, knocking down, making roads, towers and animated characters out of the blocks. Later, your child starts to experiment on their own and houses and boats begin to appear. Block building takes on a more specific focus and individual building becomes the norm.

Then, as the building becomes more complex, comes the frustration of falling blocks, missing blocks or a lack of vision, coordination or materials. You buy more blocks, keep experimenting and continue building, sometimes together and sometimes side-by-side or independently. Maybe you share little bits of block information to help with balance issues or with choosing which blocks are good to use for windows or ramps. Eventually, you look up and see architectural marvels and decide your role is now one of observer and admirer. Your child has developed the skill, confidence and motivation to work independently.

As you work with writing, keep the "block attitude". No worries. Just play, model, support and encourage. Maturity, experience and confidence will take care of the rest. Your job is to play alongside. While you play and build, understand that occasional frustration signals growth and find ways to support rather than worry or take over the process from your child. Relax and smile at changes and mistakes as they come. Children learn much faster than you can teach them. Be there, but stay out of the way.

Surround Your Child With Writing

The best way to learn a foreign language is to live with people who speak it. Just like with talking, writing is learned best when children play with it, live in it and explore how to use it without fear or limits. But unlike talking, the tools we use for writing are not part of our faces. So parents need to look closely at how they can make the tools for writing and opportunities for writing easy to access. Surround your child with people who write, reasons to write, models of writing and all the paper and pencils they can use. It is truly amazing how just a little reading and writing at home will inspire more opportunities to read and write in other places and situations as the power of writing is understood and children are ready for more. But first, just write.

Everyday Writing:
Practical, Purposeful and Powerful

The mouth is a very practical tool for the toddler. It takes in food and spills out commands without much need for outside assistance. Spoken words and sounds help children get needs met and express their wishes. For writing to progress as a natural tool with the same potential as talking, it needs to be practical, be

14

motivated by purpose, and impart power when it is used. You write so you can read later and be reminded or share a thought or a story with someone else. Grocery lists, to do lists, calendar entries, organizing labels, emails, internet searches, love notes and even palm of the hand phonebooks are all everyday needs for writing. No one checks your spelling ... or cares. The only issue is if you can remember what you wrote or sometimes, if someone else can read it. If you can do all these things in front of your child and give them the opportunity to do the same you will have a writer and a reader dressed in your child's clothes.

But how does that work when toddlers don't have the small muscle ability to write letters and if they did, the process would be too tedious? Writing is written communication. The form it takes depends on the writer. A scribble, a picture, or a letter each possess the power to communicate, hold on to information or simply slow down a memory and freeze it on a page. Playing with writing and understanding its purpose and potential is the most important part of learning to write. Since we do actually have an alphabet, letters are easily added to the mix when the purpose and power of writing are understood and children are ready for more. But first, just write.

EXPOSE the PROCESS of WRITING

Writing and reading are two sides of the same valuable coin. First of all, if you didn't read what you wrote... well that's just silly because we need each one to inform the other. Writing is a user-based activity that is dependent on reading.

Children need to see written words and experience their meaning to learn about writing. Labels inform and warn us. Signs show us where to go.

15

Picture books and novels give us insights into life. Reading makes our lives better and easier. Children also use books to learn about letters, words, sentences and the power and purpose of print.

Books, signs, cereal boxes and even tee shirts provide ways to surround your child with writing and introduce them to the purpose and magic of written symbols. Words and letters are there for a reason. Everything from a favorite store to a restroom door provides examples of the power of print. When your child understands the significance of the meaning in what is written, they see their world differently. Writing gains importance and purpose. Letters are worthy of more than a second glance.

Questions begin, as words beg to be read. So READ... everything! Signs can, obviously, be powerful and even inspire emotional responses at times.

Books Create Readers and Inspire Writers.

I still get emotional remembering my mom reading Heidi to me when I was sick with chicken pox.

The atmosphere and traditions you create by reading to your child are as important as what you read. Those shared experiences create memories and metaphors as well as making letters and words part of a happy, safe place to be.

Books also expose your child to the language of a writer. In other words, they discover that the writing in books and the way we talk can sound different. Playing with words becomes a more focused language skill. The way words are written is also presented easily through books. As your child looks at the pictures in books you can start moving your finger through the text. The left to right sweep of your hand, its orientation on the page and its movement from one page to the next is a basic skill in reading and writing that becomes automatic as a child is read to. You will find that your child eventually copies this skill. Don't worry if they go the wrong way. The more you read and they experience your modeling the more consistent their pattern will be. If there is a lot of text, just point to where you start on each page.

Don't turn your special time with a book Into a "reading lesson". It's the sharing of the moment and connecting what we read or write with who we are that makes books and people good friends. Just enjoy the book and, when you can, reveal your reading process.

Get Out the Tool Belt

If writing is going to be part of everyday life, the tools to write and read have to be accessible and livable. Think about what you will need, how to make it affordable and how to protect non-writing surfaces such as your walls from becoming petroglyphs. A basic

My granddaughter's first attempts at wanting something used the words, "Have it." No one corrected her. Instead, we sometimes adopted the same phrase when we wanted something. It was short lived and sweet. Now that her words are more conventional and specific … and demanding, we sometimes long for the simpler days of, "Have it."

start might include the following: large trays or stiff pieces of cardboard or plastic are good writing surfaces that also make it simpler to corral ongoing projects. They don't take up much room, are easy to store and still remain available by sliding them behind a chair, beside the refrigerator or next to a cabinet. Old T.V. trays work well if they aren't too heavy. Clipboards are also fascinating for young researchers.

These mobile writing surfaces also help writing move to where the action is. So whether exploring a dead bird in the back yard or an interesting event in the bathroom, the young chronicler of family events is ready, much like an 'on the scene' news reporter. Recycled paper is the easiest and cheapest thing to write on. Mistakes that are made using the printer and old mail that has a blank side that normally gets thrown away work well and keep you from worrying about the cost of creating a writer. Ask around where you work to see if you can opt to save discarded copier mistakes. A ream of printer paper is a good investment.

Pencils are the safest writing utensils to leave out on an ongoing basis. The thick yellow graphite pencils (upgraded from lead pencils of yore) work well because the point doesn't break off as easy. But they need to be kept out of easy reach of babies and toddlers who may end up writing on the roof of their mouth or beyond. Keep pencils in open containers that are easily seen and accessed by adults and older children. Crayons are safer for your child but maybe not for your walls and shoes. Make your choices work for you in a way that keeps peace and flexibility in harmony.

A plastic, or cardboard, lidded box with markers, crayons, construction paper, painter's tape and glue sticks is handy to have on hand for writing, decoration, framing, titling or book making. A toddler can see the pencils or crayons on the counter and be inspired to write. Then they can pull out the writing trays and papers before they even need adults to grab the pencils or crayons.

Inspired Materials: The materials used to write can be inspirations all on their own. Colored paper, alternate places to write, and other varied materials to write on or with, can also inspire experimenting and success with writing. Color changing, erasing and invisible markers are magic for the whole family. Crayons are easy and actually help develop finger strength because children have to push a little harder (but they get big results when they do). Writing with a stick in sand or snow or mud are also possibilities that have been explored and verified by generations of children.

MAKE WRITING PART OF OF LIVING

You probably write more than you realize. It is important for young writers to see you writing and using what you write. Instead of making your shopping list on the computer or writing it during nap time, sit on the floor with your pencil and paper and write. I do recognize how much easier this is to do without onlookers. But, really, is parenting supposed to be easy? (I happen to know that fulfilling and easy are spelled with entirely different letters.)

As you write, your child may play happily in the same room, run into the bathroom to play in the toilet or become very interested in what you are doing. If they are all over you and getting in your way, give them some paper, a pencil and something stiff to write on, if you are on carpet. Then let them scribble away.

Expose the process of writing to your child. For young children 'expose the process of writing' just means to write in front of them and talk about what you are doing. Let them watch as you think about what to write, or ask them questions to clarify what they have asked you to write.  Allow them to see you make mistakes and scratch things out without panic. You might even throw a paper away when you want to start over. It's like there is a new dog in the house and they want to watch you handle it and sense your comfort level before they are willing to try to get close to it on their own.

Do not push them to write or identify letters. Relax and just write and talk about what you write as you do it. Some children observe for a long time before they attempt anything on their own. It doesn't mean they aren't learning. They may just want a better handle on it before they venture out. (If they don't write by the time they are thirteen, just give them a spray can in the garage and their inner writer will emerge. (Not recommended.)

If You Name it, You Own It

One easy way to expose your child to print and provide examples of writing symbols is through labeling ... anywhere. Isolated alphabet letters like you see in classrooms are pretty and do provide models, but writing examples that come from your child are easy to create and much more significant because there is meaning attached to them.

You will discover many ways to write with your child. Whether the writing is taped up on a wall or lays in an open box, children will use what they write with you to influence future writing.
These inscribed papers will be their models and their inspiration as they build confidence in using pencils and words and their own ideas.

Especially when labeling, resist the urge to 'go coyote' in your home. Don't wander through the house marking all your possessions. Even a coyote tends to stick to the perimeter of his area. Too much labeling, waters down the effect of the important words in your child's world.

Let your child take the lead. Help him/her choose a letter that reminds them of what they want to say, occasionally, but encourage their independence as they show interest. Remember that a letter or two can often provide more support for future learning than a carefully lettered sign. Before they can take risks they need to gain confidence by using letters to remind them what they wanted to say.

* Try, whenever you write with children, to use lower case letters when modeling or writing in front of them. If you want to link reading and writing for your children, lower case letters will provide a more

accurate and useable example of what they see in books.

Got Picasso?

When your child creates a painting or drawing, demonstrate its importance by encouraging him/her to give it a title that can be attached. Often, parents automatically tape up their children's artwork. But taking the time to allow your child to name their piece and display that name nearby, slows down and recognizes their process of creating.

Try not to write on the artwork. Instead use a strip of paper to record its title and tape it next to the art. The title gives importance and respect to the art and the art gives the title meaning.

Associating words with their surroundings, whether in a picture, a paragraph, a book, a sign, etc., teaches your child to make sense of what they read. Three and four year olds tend to draw action pictures with stories to tell.

Labeling discussions between you and your child extend their process of creating and emphasize the importance of both what was created and the thought behind it. Simple, honest questions like, "Wow, what happened here?" "Where is the jumping part?" let children know you are listening and encourage them to think about their own thought process.

Meta-cognition (thought about thought) is an important tool for learning and using new concepts.

Associating words with their surroundings, whether in a picture, a paragraph or a book, teaches your child to make sense of what they read. Three and four year olds tend to draw action pictures and label their pictures with stories. Labeling discussions between you and your child extend their process of creating and emphasize the importance of both what was created and the thought behind it.

Other questions can also help you understand specific needs of your child. A question like, "Why did you use green?" may reveal something as ordinary as your child needs more crayons, or it may spark interest in color choice for the young Monet. Writing with your child should be a lot like play.

Fantasy Play

Child: "I bring Bunny when he eats breakfast."
Parent: "My bear is going to the bed mountain."
Child: "He has to go to store.
Parent: "Where is the store?"
Child:"In the box."

Fantasy play for even ten minutes a day can encourage positive behavior in your children all day long. I have seen this happen both at home and in the classroom. In this arena, your child is the 'master'. Children are better at fantasy play than their parents. They are able to be in control in that magical place. The child dictates the action. The parent has to pay attention or get left behind. Never reveal your lack of artistic clairvoyance. Let your child be in charge and you will be a better person for it.

Writing with your child should be a lot like play. Enjoy your time together in a world where decisions are safe to make and you can buy yourself a little wiggle room in the rules department during the rest of the day.

This is similar to what happens when children add titles or descriptions to their art. Children are the powerful ones who are in control of decision-making. They can write their name, scribble on their own or dictate for you to write.

Writing should inspire the same creativity play does, the same fun, focus and power. When you ask your child about their art, don't ask what it is. (Of course you know. It's obvious... right?) But since your mind reading abilities can sometimes be unreliable, ask, "What do you want to name it?" or say, "Tell me about it." Don't take over. Just ride your child's artistic wave.

In Antoine de Saint-Exupéry's
The Little Prince...,

... a boy draws an
elephant being eaten by
a snake. Every adult he
shows it to thinks it's a
hat. This forever changes
his opinion of adults...
and not for the better.

. . . . So don't guess............ Ask.

As available room for art on walls is depleted, or more
conventional decorating takes over, paintings and
other drawings can be cycled in and out as needed.
You decide a number for hanging and let your child
decide what pictures to use. This is also a good way
for your child to learn decision-making in a way that is
self-impacting and safe. If requests to switch paintings
come too often just set a time frame on changes, once
a week, once a month, once... Make it work for you.
Then let them add their story or title in their own words.
Or just tape their name under the picture.

Another solution to issues involving wall space is to
take a picture of the art with the label (so you
remember what it was called) and make a coffee table
art book for your child. I recommend writing the titles
in bigger print below each picture so the name stands
out and can be read and even copied in the future.
This is especially important when architecture looms its
creative head and your child panics as block building,
sheet forts and snowmen face extinction due to the
need for floor space (or warming weather).

In children's art, process is everything. By labeling,
you are not making the art better or changing it. You

are honoring it in a tangible way and extending the thinking process. As your child revisits their experience, they use the art of words to frame it. Don't be offended if your child runs off instead of talking about their project. But watch for signs of interest or comments later on that can be discussed,

Or...

...Just Listen.

Years after they were in kindergarten, I've had parents of students thank me for their child's success. To tell you the truth, what they got in my class did not make them smarter or necessarily more skilled. It was mostly an attitude they developed, an attitude that they had something to say and they had something to learn and both depended on each other. They also discovered that learning was hard work, but lots of fun. Just like play. Writing was at the center of it all.
Nurturing that attitude at home is also a very enjoyable priority.

IT'S A SIGN!

Signs are big deals. Parents stop at stop signs, are generally aware of speed limit signs and drive to many of the same signs to shop. (In fact adults may utter some of the most powerful words a child hears while looking for signs.) We use signs to inform, warn and celebrate. Sign creation can be a very powerful use of writing. Working together using signs helps older children try out their knowledge of writing. Younger children get the opportunity to contribute creatively, while having the writing process modeled. There are many possibilities for signs that are very motivating and effective ways to explore the power of print. As you experiment, you will discover what works best for your family. Our signs grew into no trespassing threats that extended to other toys and even whole bedrooms. This evolution eventually prompted a discussion of the power of our words and other, possibly less intimidating, words to protect our belongings.

Food Signs...(Menus): You tell the children the dinner menu and they come up with different names for the dishes. Their revised version of the menu can be placed on the table for general reference and discussion or copied for each diner. You may not want to do this close to Halloween, which has readily available "food" words like guts, eyeballs, and brains (unless, of course, you are dieting). Playing 'restaurant' was a favorite for my children.

Place cards: The children take turns making name cards and deciding who sits where at dinner.

Bedroom Door Signs: These are good college prep material. Dorm room doors love to be adorned with schedules, social calendar information, pleas for help and misinformation about roommates.

Bathroom Door Signs: Mostly warnings... I'd rather not elaborate.

Ownership Signs: Some possibilities here are names, or scribbled versions thereof, penned on disposable cups or scratched in the dirt denoting property rights in play yards or even etched on tree limbs for spying. No Trespassing

Pet Signs: Pets have names and only parents in danger of having their credentials revoked don't know them. But it can be difficult to stay informed when pets change names due to the whim of the owner or because Happy the Hamster suddenly became Speedy the Runaway... (start looking). Of course, when the pet eats the sign it provides yet another writing opportunity.

Organizational Signs: Labels for toy bins and shelves can be created and used by children or adults.

Labels for Creative Play: Writing can be incorporated into block creations, theater set-ups, scavenger hunts, forts or bakery shelves for mud pies, rock creations or experiments (save yourself, don't ask) ... Be creative.

Lovable Signs: A favorite family phrase or words of love can be posted on a bedpost or a bedroom wall for special occasions or maybe a nighttime reminder of safety or love. When my daughter was afraid of the dark we made a sign for her bedroom wall with a verse about God keeping David safe when he slept.

Lists, Letters & Notes

The lists children make are important to them, so don't scribble things out yourself. Let your child use a fancy crayon or marker to make their own deletions on the list decorative and fun. Remember, these lists are not binding, no matter what your tiny 'list tyrant' says.

Shopping Lists

If you are writing a shopping list and your children have experience watching and listening to you as you have made previous lists, ask your children if they want a certain item. If they are interested, ask them to write (or scribble) it on your list or make one of their own. Talk about the list. Read their item and point to it. When you go to the store ask your child to read the item they wrote. No pressure! If they say nothing, say, "Was that 'vegetables'? Thanks for putting it on the list so I would remember it." (Okay, fine. Say what they really wrote, not what you really want. Unless you are into manipulation under the guise of writing.)

Let your child help put it in the basket or hold on to it. Of course, depending on what it is they might eat it as well and cause a scene at checkout. As they become aware of things during the week that are needed, encourage them to put them on their list. Then when you go to the store they can use their own list to remind you what to buy.

Find an accessible area for shopping lists. I had a clip magnet for each child on the refrigerator, but a box on a counter or inside a low cupboard would work just as well. Choose a place that is accessible and safe from dogs and the more mouth oriented members of your family.

This process of making lists helps diffuse begging as well. When they say they want something, have them put it on their list. Then, later, you can see if you already have it and show them so they can cross it off their list or it stays on to be used as a reminder at the store. It is surprising how much young ones remember from their list of scribbles. If they don't remember, you can also just move on and the item may come up later and spark their memory. You may also find that just having a list to scribble on is all your child needs to feel important at this point, meaning may actually be irrelevant.

As they get older, children may copy the names on used up boxes onto their list. The more important a list item is, the more attention the child will give to recording it. For instance, candy may have many big important letters while milk or cheese may just barely be symbolically represented.

The Family that Writes Together...
Needs Pencils

Maybe a to-do list? Ask if there is something your children want to do during the day and add it to your to-do list. Again, write it and read it to them or let them scribble their request on your list (or their own list) and read it to you. There is something about writing on mommy's or daddy's paper that is magical. Then, as you do things on the list, show them how the list helped you remember. Then encourage them to read what they, or you, wrote and check it off or scratch it out. This can also grow into your child's own list of hopes for the day. Of course, even though being on the list gives an item some power, you don't have to act on everything on the list. For instance, cutting their own hair (or mommy's or the dog's) or taking a bath with the TV remote or the cat, although fun ideas, are (fortunately for us all) still subject to adult approval.

The Postal Service is Your Friend

If you are writing a "thank you" card, let your children watch you write and read it to them or verbalize as you write. Then ask your children what they want to say. Have them write some letters and read it back to you. They can also add a picture while you write a dictation or title to go with it. Cards can also be created entirely by your child with lots of important scribbles and letters. Depending on the card recipient's ability to decipher squiggles and lines, you might want to send the card 'as is' or add a piece of paper with a more conventionally written translation.

Even play dates, can be enhanced by writing. For the price of a postage stamp your child can scribble a note inviting a friend to a play date you, of course, have already set up unbeknownst to the children.

Your child gets to write, their friend gets to read and the anticipation begins.

While you are at it, encourage relatives and friends to write to your children. Playmates also make great pen pals. The best letters are short on words (a sentence or two is plenty) and occasionally contain something like a sticker or picture or small treat. I write letters to my granddaughter who lives in another state. When she visited our home over the holidays she was so enamored with our big plastic candy canes that I decided to mail a small edible one in my next letter. When the letter arrived it held two recognizable candy cane pieces and a lot of magic candy cane dust. My son said my granddaughter licked the envelope clean and requested another visit to the mailbox ... just in case.

Everyday Needs & Events

We all need reminders. Children are natural note takers and memo writers. The amount of writing needed in this setting is small and very suited to a youthful attention span. Every whine is a potential memo.

Child: "I want candy!"
Adult: "Write that down so you remember."

Writing provides a way to calm down the intensity of wants and demands (usually interchangeable words) while teaching the power of writing. Big sticky notes work well, or recycled paper, maybe some tape and a place to put the notes. For example, if your toddler wants you to find her toy, ask her to write you a note so you will remember. She can scribble on a paper and leave you a note. When you finish what you are doing, take the note for her to read to you. By then she has probably found the toy or, more likely, found another toy to play with, but she knows you remembered to come because of her writing. Leaving a note becomes a promise between the two of you to address each situation. Keep in mind, addressing the situation does not mean doing as ordered, it means giving attention to the problem.

Notes are short and simple, and have no formal expectations. We have a tradition with notes at our house. It started when I slipped notes in backpacks when my baby, toddler and kindergartner went to Daddy's on Friday nights. Before they could read, I read the notes to them ahead of time so each written thought could just sit in the backpack and do its magic. Then came lunch box notes. On April Fools' Day, lunch notes might have resided between slices of bread but they were eventually found before being totally ingested. Reminder notes are also useful because they are much more effective and less emotionally scarring than nagging.

Even when my children couldn't read, the notes were exciting reminders of safety that could be taken to a sibling or adult to be read. Early in the school year my kids' pockets held a little note from mom, a Disney character, or sometimes the dog, to be read or just held during a long day away from home. When my children went on trips I wanted the notes to last a long time so I hid them in random clothing.

During the day, stuff happens...

If any of that stuff is important to your child or needs sharing with a busy or absent parent, grandparent or sibling write it down with your child. Ask your child what happened and write down what they dictate. Then let them illustrate it and/or share it with someone who was absent for the event at a later time. Your children will eventually want to do the writing themselves as they get used to the concept. A scribble is all they need to help them remember. Then let them tape the note to a door or put it on a table or in a box so the information will not be forgotten. Later, your child can take on the role of reader as they relay the information. These reports may include stories of broken toys, skinned knees, mud sculptures, new teeth, lost teeth, play dates, dog throw up, new bugs or may simply be 'I love you,' notes. In this way your child experiences the role of writing in remembering and caring for others.

The following note was for the doctor. We still have the attached signed note that took the focus off the fear that day.

Translation: *Tell me if it will hurt.*
Sign right up. No.....Yes
(The doctor checked "NO")

Voting experiences can involve short written responses and effectively display the power of print by influencing family decisions. Only use voting if you are prepared to live with the outcome. Which is why clear instructions are important. As children get older and engage in short periods of lobbying for their preferred choices, they hone their verbal abilities to persuade (and prepare for the LSAT).

New pet: .... Tarantula or Frog?
Book to read: .... Scary or Funny?
Game to Play: .... Dominos or Candy Land?
Pizza toppings: ...... Pepperoni or Cheese?
Outing: .... Park or Friend's house?

The way you vote can also inspire children to use and remember letters and connect them to writing. For example they could write a 'P' for park or an 'F' for friend. 'Muppets or Madonna' might pose a problem. ('MP', 'MA'?) Children can help count votes as they read and sort the letters. Families might want to allow multiple voting just to make it interesting. If you are the manipulative sort, bribing for votes may even work. "Every toy you pick up gives you a vote on the lunch menu." You still decide on choices for the vote you can live with and your children end up writing letters over and over as they cast and count the votes.

(Any prison time served for multiple voting as an adult, stemming from childhood voting habits, is not the responsibility of the author.)

Surveys can also encourage and enlighten your beginning researcher. Just draw a line down the middle of a paper (preferably on a clipboard for the most professional look) and let your child decide what they want to find out. The ideas can come from anyone, but are more motivating if they grow out of something going on in the family. Responses from siblings, parents or even family pets can be recorded in the appropriate column for later reports. This can be very similar to voting. Maybe one side of the paper has a 'CH' for chocolate and the other a 'V' for vanilla. You can find out about family preferences or decide on a dessert. A wider survey might involve phone calls to other relatives and friends for their opinions. As with voting, math comes into the picture as well. Of course, more lines down the paper allow for more survey choices. Favorites are easy topics for early survey experiences (i.e. favorite colors, animals, pizza toppings, cereals, egg preparations, books, movies).

A ringing phone must trigger some primal need in children to talk to their parents. It seems to be a child magnet. Can you hear the stampede?

(The Pied Piper must have had a cell phone. Maybe he was a time traveler?) When you are on the phone seems to be the time when your children suddenly realize there are important things you need to know about or questions you need to answer. As mentioned before, writing provides a way to slow down pieces of your life and give you and your child both time to think. Just keep pencil and paper handy.

A Tradition of Notes: My youngest son was seriously dating a sweet young woman to whom he is now married. She came to visit when my husband and I were out of town, and stayed in our house. I left notes all over the house to try and help her feel welcomed in a strange place. When we returned after she left, we spent a week being surprised by her notes each time we opened a new cabinet.

My older son spent a year studying (?) in a foreign country and met his future wife (studying?). My, now, daughter-in-law told me that my son left "half a million notes" for her to find after he left to return to the United States.

No matter what children write (or how they write) they have usually said what they wanted to say several times upon entering the room. The paper allows you to delay answering and allows children to relay information and learn to wait. Thus, you stay in control of your time.

Apparently, children have figured out something we all know. It's like asking your boss if you can do something when she/he are extremely busy with something else. You often get an answer that's less thought out and more convenient for you. A lot can be said for asking questions when someone is busy. Not that I would have ever done that myself, but I'm just sayin'...

A spiral notebook with a clipped pen close by for emergencies, or phone calls or visitors, can be helpful. As the children get a little older you can even write a response if one is really necessary at that moment. Mostly a simple written, "Yes," or "No."

Children love to cook and recipes provide a great way for children to use reading and writing. Cooking ties print, and the need for accurate reading to the real world in a very tangible way. If that world includes chocolate, it's even better.

Even very young children learn a lot from helping their parent crack eggs and pour and stir ingredients as mommy or daddy model the importance of reading by pointing to the recipe and following the instructions. This is a very towel-worthy activity that also requires extra ingredients to be on hand to replace excitable eggs or fluttery flour that escape the bowl.

Ambidextrous parents tend to have the most success but highchairs can help even the playing field. Pictures of the cooking experiences help you smile again at the memories created.

My children also thought it was cheating to use someone else's recipe. Cooking was more like experimenting to them. But the recipes they created were very important (and sometimes repulsive to those asked to taste). A pencil and a recipe notebook were always needed to record and later edit or duplicate their culinary attempts.

Rules are important
when experimenting in the kitchen.

First, parents need to be sure that only items safe to ingest are available in kitchen cabinets, which have not been childproofed. Second, no recipes can require the use of knives. When my kids were young I would put out small amounts of requested products on the kitchen table along with plastic bowls, measuring equipment, cooking utensils and writing implements. We would talk as they worked and I managed the heating issues.

When they recorded their "recipes", they copied names of ingredients off bottles and jars or just wrote the important letters they heard. Sometimes I was called upon to identify unlabeled substances like flour and sugar. As they were able to reach the spice shelves these "recipes" became very expensive! Years later I found labeled plastic bags, holding small bowls containing cooking projects, which included ice-bound spoons, in the back of my freezer. (So that's where the spoons disappeared to!) Whether using or creating a recipe, writing and reading become hands-on tools. The language of math is also expanded in the kitchen as teaspoon and cup, as well as degrees and time segments, are used for important purposes.

Celebrate With Writing

Holidays and special events are natural motivators for writing. This type of writing lends itself to family traditions and recorded memories. These examples are from our holidays but the same ideas can be used for any family celebrations or traditions.

Cards and books are great gifts for children to make. My son wrote a book about a raccoon to give a friend of ours who took him to a baseball game. The friend has treasured that book now for almost 20 years. My granddaughter's holiday gifts this year were cards she made with her name letters and snowman sticker pieces strewn about a piece of cardboard. Get out paper, markers, crayons, stickers and whatever art supplies are hanging around your laundry room and help your child create sweet personal gifts that don't cause stress and demonstrate the importance of your child's own creative process.

Lists and letters are real winners for writing opportunities during holidays. Birthday and holiday wish lists may be very selfishly oriented BUT they are big motivators. Children pay close attention to toys and their boxes. The toys provide motivation and the boxes are full of print. Fancy, big, colorful letters abound.

(Luckily for the manufacturers, children can't read most of the small print on the boxes, or toys might no longer be motivators.)

During some holidays, parents are barraged with requests from their children as the kids worry that their parents might not remember their specific suggestions for gift purchasing.

> **Keeping danger out of the kitchen (and the neighbors' kitchens) can be part of your role in the literacy of your children. So be sure to establish good relationships in your neighborhood.**
>
> My youngest son worked in the kitchen alone one day and then asked me if he could sell his 'experiment' to the neighbors. He showed me a cardboard box with six yogurt cups. Each cup had a note on top, "Experiment 25¢," spelled in four year old spelling. I asked him what they were. He said, "Experiments," (Mom can't read?) and took one out, shook it, and put it in the sink.
> Then he stood back.
> We waited silently for a few seconds until the top popped off of the yogurt container. That was it. After I put more baking soda and vinegar on my shopping list I sent him off to the homes of a few specific, easily duped neighbors while I stood in the doorway. He came back with $1.25 after only going to two houses. He ran out of 'experiments'. It was his first experience dealing in chemicals as well as his first experience with public funding. Luckily, his adult career took a different route.

Writing activities can help relieve the panic your children feel as gift giving celebrations approach and calm the immediate tension created by TV and paper ads presenting new toys that, "Any parent who truly loves their child would love to purchase at unbelievably low prices."...?

Remember, writing has the ability to slow things down. Writing also puts responsibility in the hands of the writer. So grab the notebooks and let your children "WANT" on paper.

Vacations also build memories.

No matter where you go, remembering what happens on a vacation is a good thing. You may be thinking, "But we have had some terrible vacations." Aha, that's exactly the point. The memories we tend to retell and laugh about the most later on are the things that didn't go as planned. Both good and bad memories are just part of the experience.

All you need is a spiral notebook (they are very cheap, especially around back to school time) and a click pen. Don't worry about the lined paper in the notebooks. Young children easily ignore and write across the lines. When they are ready, the lines take on more significance. Click pens are nice because you can close them up when your child is through and the points don't generally break, like pencils can.

Vacations are great opportunities for learning. You don't have to go anywhere expensive. Camping is like crawling into the biggest, best science classroom ever. Visits to Aunt Lilly's house may force you to hear all your childhood stories ... again, but your children hear the stories and see themselves in a different way and gain new insight into their family. Write about these times and encourage your children to do the same. Then encourage your children to draw and, later, paste photos of moments they want to save. Of course, I wouldn't let Aunt Lilly find your notebook. (Spiral notebooks survive this well.)

Story Writing

If children want to write a story on their own, ask them what they want to write about. Little ones may tell their story in one rambling flow of consciousness and need to write it as one big swirly picture to talk about when they read.

But if your child tells the story in segments, ask what comes first and maybe what would be next. Then encourage them to put just one sentence or thought on each page as they write their story. This helps them limit each page to one idea and makes it easier for them to read and maybe illustrate later on.

My children wrote at different times during vacations. Sometimes they would pull their notebooks out of their backpacks and draw or write while we drove. These writings included anything from scenery or lunch vignettes to angry pictures or comments about a sibling stealing a fruit snack.

If we got to our destination early enough, we would all relax and write or draw to calm down before bed and give mom a chance to get organized. Most writing occurred at the end of the day as they recapped various adventures. We didn't write every night, just when we had time and some ideas. One of my sons wrote the word 'REMEMBER' in huge letters on certain pages just to emphasize his desire to reread about that particular day after we got home.

If they write more than one thought on a page it becomes confusing for them to read. When they get confused, they become dependent. A big part of a child's confidence and success in writing lies in controlling and remembering what they have written.

The way pages are put together can also help story writers gain even more control of their writing. One way to do this is to show them how to glue the story pages to each other, top to bottom, so they create a continuous sheet of paper (like a scroll). This way, the pages stay in order and can be seen as a connected story by your child. If your child decides to make changes, pages can be easily cut apart and re-glued in a new location. This process of gluing pages helps your child to see each idea separately and yet attached to the bigger story. They can physically see their story grow and change. These stories can be cut apart and stapled into book form or typed after the child has written them, read them and played with them.

Here is one way to help children make this transition from handwritten to typed text. Type each page to be identical with each written page. Then add matching page numbers to both the written and the typed pages. Now the typed pages can be illustrated independently. Their own 'child readable' handwritten pages help them know what to draw on the new typed pages. Then your child can match page numbers and staple it all together to make a book. The illustrations can give them clues to help them read as they move away from their handwritten pages. All the time they spend playing with their words, matching the typed pages to their writing and drawing pictures to match the words on each typed page helps them gain independence as they now read their book with confidence.

BOOK MAKING

"Creativity is intelligence having fun." Albert Einstein

Anything important enough to talk about can be made into a book. Even some things you would rather not talk about can be interesting topics. Books can be created a variety of ways. The more involved and interested the child is in the topic, the more time can be spent on it. Simple books that suit the moment may be read for only one day or kept for a lifetime.

Several sentences or words dictated about a topic might be written on separate pages and illustrated. Or a series of labeled pictures might get together for a literary moment. A book can consist of anything that the author wants to draw or write about.

Book Production Ideas:
How you choose to put a book together depends on the author's needs, available materials and storage possibilities.

Museum Collections: An author of any age could lay each page of their book on the floor so the author and friends can discuss each work of art. These can be kept in individual folders or bags for future display purposes.

Paper and Stapler: Your stapler is your friend. You can assemble most any stack of thin materials easily to make books (i.e. paper, light plastic, material, paper sack)

Sewn Books: If you cut a bunch of rectangles out of material with pinking shears you will have the basics for several kinds of books. Since markers bleed through material, make your rectangles big enough to be folded into two pages. Then fold them with cardboard in between in order to write and draw. Then sew all the ends together and read. I am not a seamstress and I am seriously, artistically challenged so I will leave the beautification of the books to you.

Books for Baby: Parents can draw or trace pictures on the pages of material books and label them. You can even sew on extra material for textured pages or use textured materials for the pages.

Shape Books: The hard part about shape books is figuring out a shape that is possible to cut that your child can recognize. Luckily, the two of you will talk it over first so your chances of approval are higher. You can make these books several ways. One method is to cut the cover of the book in the appropriate shape and cut the other pages smaller to fit.

* Or you can trace the cover you just cut on all the pages so every page is the same throughout the book. This is my preferred way to do it because as your child writes, draws or scribbles on the pages they are reminded of the topic. This brings us back to the importance of the shape being recognizable. You can also make every page a different shape.

<u>Paper Plate Books:</u> They work well for babies and toddlers because they are more chew resistant than paper sheets and easier to work with than material. Little ones can scribble or draw on both sides of individual paper plates. Then the assortment of plates can be scooped together and tied with a SHORT string that can't be untied and wrapped around a neck. Adults can add words or pictures or nothing at all and let the mauling begin!

<u>Giant Books:</u> Large books can be made out of butcher paper, plastic tablecloths, sheets, cardboard pieces, boxes or basically anything large. (I'll bet you didn't see that one coming.) Individual words or sentences can also be spread out over an entire room or house on individual sheets of paper to celebrate an important event.

<u>Shoeboxes:</u> Shoes were actually invented to create something to do with shoeboxes other than using them for decorating and storing special trinkets. Even if actual shoes are stored in them they can still be used to store information on the outside. The stories of shopping or needs for new shoes are as varied as the feet they encase. Whatever the story, it can be recorded on the box and remembered each time the shoes are worn.

<u>Large Boxes:</u> Appliance boxes are lots of fun to write and draw on. They can be forts or houses or caves or just hiding places. Ownership signs or stories of the adventures that go on inside can make for exciting reading and illustrating later. Be sure to take pictures. (They are precious

memories that can do double duty during the teen years as blackmail.) It is also amazing how small a box a child can fit into.

This information might even help you childproof your house so tiny spaces for getting stuck aren't ignored.

Boxes etc.: Toy boxes already have a reputation for eliciting more creative play than the toys they contain. So use them to your advantage. When your child has something to say about the toy, write it down and stick it on the box. OR use the pictures on the box as labeling opportunities. OR cover the whole box and use each side to tell part of a story. OR use it as a giant die to roll for games with dots or pictures or names. You get the idea. Play with it.

Calendar Books: Old calendars are cheap and bound and big beautiful pictures are already there to be explored and revised with a little help from a crayon or marker. Glue a sheet of paper over the dates for your child's writing about the pictures. (Continued on page 49)

Dear Tooth Fairy, Don't let Jacob see this letter! Right when I wrote this Jacob was saying, "Woo-wee Boo-bee to his cabbage patch. This time I'm going to be a rip off, give me $2.00 or your head.

This is my personal collage of evidence concerning the abuse of fantasy characters in previously well-meaning traditions. Sweet memories as teenagers take new paths.

Dear Tooth fairs (momma),

Don't let Jacob see this letter! right when I wrote ~~this~~ this Jacob was saying "Woo-Wee Boo-Bee" to his cabb e patch. This time I'm going to be a rip-off, give me 2.00 or your head.

| Please Respond |

Der ㅜata kos, I do not IF EOPEL PEsSMAHN

Dear Tooth Fairy, Enclosed are three teeth that I have painfully lost. But there is another one, but the pressure in the washcloth I put it in destroyed it. I would like it if you gave me credit for it anyways. Thanks!

Dear Tooth fairy,
                    Three
Enclosed are ~~two~~ teeth
that I have painfully lost.
But there is another
one, but the pressure
in the wash cloth
I pat it in, destroyed it
I would like it if you
gave me credit for it
any ways. I hate!

48

On vacations, a calendar of the area where you are staying can make a great travel book. (How do you think Rick Steves got his start?) Different family members can comment on the same page or choose their own page for comments.

Calendars have themes. If you find a calendar about a topic your child is interested in, bring it home for a research project. For instance, if the theme is cats, encourage your child to look closely at the pictures and see what new thing they can discover about cats on each page (e.g. whiskers, colors, ear shapes, things they like to do, eye colors, how they sit or stand or jump).

Bathtub Books: There are several companies that make bathtub crayons. They can be used to draw or write funny words or random letters. You might even write a short story for your child to find on the wall of the tub or shower when bath time rolls around. Just focus on fun and meaning.

Sidewalk Books: Sidewalk chalk is great for creating giant bears with growling sounds coming out of their mouths or labeled fish or family members. Try to stay away from caricatures of the neighbors...unless you are moving.

Hard Cover Books:

There are lots of options for making hard cover books. All you need are two sheets of something stiff like cardboard or tag board, something to wrap around the stiff pieces and a plan for attaching that cover to the pages of the book. An easy combination of materials to use is cereal box cardboard pieces and contact paper. One way to cover the book is to staple the book pages together with two blank pages on the outside. Then just leave enough space between the cardboard pieces when you lay them on the contact paper to allow you to place the edges of the pages between the cardboard pieces. Glue the two blank outside pages on to each corresponding cardboard piece. Then wrap the outside edges of the contact paper around the cardboard and over the glued outside pages of the book.

Computer Books:

Use a program where pictures are easily inserted and text can be moved around as well. After your child has dictated or written a story on paper, type it on the computer and either print off the typed pages for your child to illustrate or let them decorate them on the computer before printing. Computerized books and cards are also fun to send to friends and relatives. It is beneficial for a young child to see their story written on paper first if possible.

Online Books:

There are many online book-publishing sites that are fun to use. The books are a little pricey but the product is unbeatable for something important. They make great gifts and memory keepers. You can scan drawings or photos or writing and label them with captions or short dictated stories. Or you might illustrate a single continuous story over several pages. Organize posed pictures with friends, family members or even stuffed animals or toys and capture them on camera to make the book a group project. Make a book about your children to be cherished by recipients.

Look for a program that gives you a lot of flexibility. Make sure you can adjust pictures and resize print to be large enough for the eyes of young children. Large print is especially important for easy reading by little ones.

WHAT YOU KNOW YOU WANT TO ASK

"My spelling is wobbly. It's good spelling but it wobbles, and the letters get in the wrong places."
A. A. Milne (author of Winnie the Pooh)

Alphabet Letters

It may seem that the names and the order of letters in the alphabet aren't really needed except to alphabetize, because the sounds, not the names of letters, are used to write. But if you look a little closer you realize that most of the letters have names that yell out their sound for all to hear. So I've learned that talking about and playing with the letters can be helpful. This is not to be confused with testing letter names to show grandma that your child can learn. Of course your darling child can learn. Didn't she learn to flush her bear down the toilet? Color on walls? Use every bad word you never uttered out loud? When letters become test materials they lose their powers and work against the long-term goal of creating lifelong readers and writers. This is actually the dark side of the alphabet. Stay clear of alphabet abuse. Love and pet the letters. Talk about them and notice things about what they look like and how their names sound. Young children learn through investigation and play, so focusing on memorization is a real waste of their time and yours. Don't test. Play.

Spelling

If your child asks you how to spell a word, what do you do? If your child already plays with letters in their writing, say, "Write a letter that will help you remember the word." Sometimes this letter isn't even in the same country as any of the sounds in the word. No worries. The whole idea is to understand that the letters are there to remind the reader. If your child is satisfied, then so are you. Right?

Isolating and Using Sounds

Never help a child spell a word they haven't already written. If help is still requested after they write something, ask, "What sound do you hear?" not, "What letter ...." This is important because hearing and isolating sounds in words is a necessary part of writing and learning to spell. The sound your child hears may be one sound from a whole phrase or sentence rather than from a word. Go ahead and celebrate that sound with a letter.

Sometimes you will need to help them isolate a sound. Listen to them say the word or say it with them and listen for a sound they are able to hold on to. They will usually start by hearing a dominant sound or a beginning or ending sound. Sometimes just holding on to the last sound in a word is easiest.

If your child isn't really ready to isolate a sound yet, back up. It is hard to move forward when you don't know where you are. Help your child appreciate what they can do. Encourage them to use any letter they think will remind them of what they wanted to say. Or they may just want to copy letters. Keep writing fun and make sure they are successful. Be honest and validate their efforts by identifying and respecting what they do. Instead of focusing on sounds and words, say, "What letter/s would you like to write?" Then let them have fun copying random letters. They are still in control because they know what they are doing. They are copying letters they like. It's not writing, but it is still art. Children are the masters of pretend. Be honest or they will figure you out.

When children are ready to use letters and sounds and adults spell for them, instead of letting children do the work by listening for and isolating sounds, writing stays in its own little magic writing club and children feel excluded. The letters stay magical (not understood). If your child can isolate a sound they hear, they have figured something out independently. Then you can help show them how the letter looks that goes with that sound. It's sort of like introducing them to a new friend from the writing club. Eventually, the members of the club will be out walking the streets having meaningful conversations with your child because the mystery is gone and the club doors are thrown open.

Spelling can easily set up a tiny writing dictatorship that surrounds letters and sounds with so many rules and fear that it limits your child's growth. This is an important point because I have seen children so fearful of writing the wrong letters that they lose confidence and stop writing. I have also seen survivors learn the system at an early age but then have trouble moving beyond spelling. Meaning and creativity take a back seat.

A child who plays with writing and uses writing effectively can always learn rules as they mature. Then they can welcome those rules into their world rather than be limited by them in a world they are just beginning to grab hold of. Conventional spelling develops later as children start editing what they write and begin to memorize words they use consistently. Only at that point is it helpful for your child to begin learning how spelling works. Help your child to create, not worry.

One Letter, One Word

Your child does not need to use lots of letters. When children really start getting comfortable with reading and writing, using one sound for each word helps them get a handle on how words work. They can point to words (letters) and read what they wrote. If they put more than one letter for a word they may still try to point to a new letter for each word they say and get lost.

If you try to get them to leave spaces between words at this point, I guarantee that when they write independently you will have a bunch of letters with random spacing unrelated to individual words. They need to be able to see letters in groups, as word units, before you worry about spaces. Once they have a good handle on "one letter, one word" they can start adding to their one-letter words by keeping all the letters for a word almost stuck together. If you just focus on putting letters for a word close together the spacing will come.

As your child keeps writing, more common words become word units to them. If their writing shows they are ready for help with spelling, here are some things to watch for as you offer 'helpful' assistance for your child.

Five Rules

1 – Talk about spelling only if your child is already comfortable with writing and then reading their own writing and uses letters and sounds easily.

> Translation: Wait until they are ready.

2 – Only help them spell words they have already written in a completed thought.

> Translation: Stop hovering.

3 – Only spell words that are asked for.

> Translation: Be polite.

4 – Let your child decide whether or not to edit words they have written.

> Translation: Whose writing is it?

5 – Stop before you overstay your welcome.

> Translation: No offense, but enough is enough.

This kind of spelling with children works because they have already thought about what they wanted to say and have written it down. Of course spelling matters, but not when you are four ... or five...or have 'spell check'. The more your child understands the power of writing and has experience with creating meaning with words, the more they will want to make sure they can read what they write. Then, how their writing looks so it can be read by others later gains more importance.

When you worry about spelling, remember that children do not fixate on bad spelling anymore than they fixated on saying, "Wah wah," for water every time they got thirsty as a baby. Your child has been growing and changing since they were born. Why would that stop with spelling? Relax.

Phonics

Babies laugh or cry for a reason even if we don't know what it is. They make sounds that cause things to happen. Parents respond to sounds and look for meaning. When your child says, "Mamma," or, "Dada," they get hugged and kissed. "Dink," might produce a bottle. As a parent you would find it silly if you were told to teach those precious sounds separate from what they are meant to express. Talking relies on this fusion of sound and meaning and so does writing. Writing is a lot like talking. Meaning, sounds, experiences and lots of other language clues should all live happily together to create meaning.

Phonics connects letters and sounds. People tend to think of phonics when they think about reading and writing. Isolating phonics away from reading/writing changes it into something that is no longer reading or writing at all. Phonics is a tool that is productive when used with other skills for meaning.

Many languages use sounds and letters for reading and writing. Those sounds and letters are one part of what goes on between a person and a text. The person and their surroundings and history play with the text to make meaning.

Writing and reading are actually something like chemical reactions where the components change to be something altogether different, unrecognizable as what they were before. Like H_2O, an H or an O by itself just isn't water. The H and the O's are totally different by themselves. They need to be together just to stay in a glass, much less a lake or an ocean. You can't learn about water from studying hydrogen and oxygen. Writing is much more involved and multidimensional than that. Talking about water made me thirsty, so go get a cold glass of water and meet me back here. While you're at it get one for your child.

Reading Children's Writing

Trying to read children's writing back to them can make you feel like you have gone to the 'dark side'. Visions of hurt feelings and parent inadequacy spring out of hidden places. Oh, for the good old days of secret decoder rings in cereal boxes!
My policy is that the writer does the reading.
So if your child brings you anything from a sheet of squiggles to a piece of writing with almost legible sentences and asks you to read it, you say the same thing each time. "You read it because you wrote it." Then just sit and wait. Make it a privilege and expectation for them to read their work, not a guessing game for panicked adults. Remember, reading is part of writing. Don't deprive your child of the opportunity to depend on his/her own writing to read. That's part of the magic and the benefit of writing.

WRITING DOS AND DON'TS
Writing Dos

No matter how many dictionary pages you had to copy or "I will nots" you had to write in school, please DO not pass this experience on to your children. If you want your child to write an apology for something, let him/her draw a picture or talk face to face. The only "mistake" a young writer makes is not being able to read what they write. This is where you need to encourage your children to use whatever letters help them remember.

* Talk about what is going to be written.
* Always pay attention to
    the meaning of whatever is written.
* Always let your <u>child</u> "read"
    what has been written

Writing Don'ts:
* Writing should never be tedious for children. If it seems tedious, speed up or stop or get busy somewhere else, whichever works best in the situation. Often when adults leave, children are more resourceful because no one is looking over their shoulders. Doesn't it work the same way for adults? One advantage of writing is you can always come back to it ... or it wasn't that important.
* Don't correct "mistakes" just help your child use what he/she knows or asks you about to create writing more readable for your child.
* Never never use writing as punishment!

ERASERS

Young children don't use erasers well.
Erasers are a waste of time for little
ones for several reasons.

1. Erasing gives appearance more importance than thinking on a child's paper.
2. Erasing takes up more time and wastes more paper with eraser drilled holes than just crossing out changes.
3. Erasures make writing hard to read because tiny fingers can't erase well enough without drilling through the paper. Words written on top of erasures are hard to read.
4. Erasing hides editing. As children change their writing to make it more interesting, factual or readable, the places they cross out memorialize their growth as a writer. In my kindergarten and first grade classes we called crossed out places 'think marks' because they displayed that the children were thinking.

COMPUTERS

For young ones who are interested in being on
your lap when you use the computer but don't
yet understand the difference between the
computer and a giant LEGO, there are baby safe
programs available. The ones I currently know of
lock up normal key functions and, instead, show flying,
colorful pictures of letters and shapes when keys are
hit.

Computer video calling programs also offer a good way to familiarize your child with the computer in a positive way. Your child can fill chat boxes with letters and shapes while talking to others. The computer can also be used to print out names or other words of interest for a toddler's eager scribbles.

Talk to your child about the computer. Let them see it used in varied situations, not just for computer games. Let them explore the computer as a tool to write, draw, look up pictures and talk to relatives and friends. Be creative and so will they.

GROWING WRITING TOGETHER

"To me the greatest pleasure of writing is not what it's about, but the music the words make." Truman Capote

Children gain experience and confidence with their own writing in nurturing home environments. But then impending school age looms. Parents who were previously relaxed become a bit tense as their confidence dwindles in the face of school demands. Mom and Dad begin having problems with self worth and their lack of preparation for HOMEWORK and REPORT CARDS.

Actually, the time you spend going on walks and talking about nests in the trees and why it feels funny when you put a key in the electric outlet (another story) is the best preparation

you can give your child for their school years. Reading, communicating, interacting with nature, talking about how things work, building, cooking, caring for others and excitement about learning are more important for creating good readers, writers and scholars than memorization of alphabet letters and spelling rules.

What happens next?

Instead of running out to buy workbooks and destroying the good feelings about writing and reading you have instilled in your child, you can just formalize some of the things you are already doing. Remember, like Jack, of beanstalk fame, don't go looking for the cow when the magic beans are already in your possession. You want to open the world up to your child. So don't settle for anything less. Enjoy the process of writing together.

Clues From Your Child

Your clue to knowing if your child is ready to tackle something new in writing, is when they start having problems reading what they write after they were previously comfortable. If they just don't like the way it looks or want someone else to do it, they probably only need more encouragement and confidence, not more skills. Otherwise, occasional frustration when they are writing most likely indicates that they are ready for more.

This is one place where the interdependence of reading and writing really shows up. Often what happens is your child's ability to read begins to out distance their ability to write. So for their own sake as a reader, they have to incorporate more of what they need for reading into their writing. As their experiences with books, pencils and paper reveal more of this relationship between writing and reading, they view their writing differently and ask more specific questions.

> ### Write: from a kindergartener autobiography
> *"Writing is totally fun for me. That's why I write. Writing is so easy for me. You see so much stuff when you write. When you ride in the car you don't worry about rocks and nails. You look out the window. You see trees, houses, restaurants and people. You listen to music and chew bubble gum. But you don't worry."*

"What letter goes Buh?" "Do I need more letters?" "What is this 'K' for?" "Where does it say, 'Ride'?" Just answer the questions as asked and help your child use the information while you answer. You don't need to help beyond what they ask for. Teachable moments are called teachable moments because they are moments (short) focusing on your child wanting a skill or piece of information that has a practical use in that moment (short). Any discussion beyond what they ask about is generally a waste of time.

The Roles of Revision and Editing
Revision and editing are important tools that help your children gain control of their writing. As your children go back to what they have written to make it more readable or change what they said or how they said it, they gain power over it. It's not like when you were in school and you had to revise or edit to please a teacher.

When children revise their writing, they take control of the content. When they edit, they make their writing easier to read for themselves and others. Revising and editing need to be tools for meaning, not for pleasing. If your child is worried about approval, meaning gets buried in fear and limited by spelling and punctuation. This process of specifically working on writing starts with editing. But it is important that the requests for editing come from your child. This process begins naturally when they can't read what they write.

Your role is to keep referring to what they wanted to say as you sort it out together. First, obviously, ask what they wanted to say. If they can't remember, there are several things you can do and they concern the piece of paper in their hand. Use whatever fits the situation. The point, early on is to depend on letters, even if only one letter is used for an entire paragraph.

Dependance on letters is the goal that will create a confident writer and reader.

*Ask them what they were thinking about when they were writing.

* Have them look at the paper and see if there are any letters there that remind them of what they wanted to say.

* Maybe point to some specific letters and ask about them."Here is a 'B' at the beginning. Did your idea start with (sound of 'B') sound?"

* If they remember what it was about but can't remember the words, ask where an important word is. Help them notice the letters they used that might be good candidates to help them find the word. "It's about the worms we played with? What sound do you hear in worm? Say it slow and listen. Okay keep making that sound. What letter makes that sound? Is there a letter on your paper that could make that sound?"

* If even the topic eludes them, suggest that they take their writing back to where they were working and see if that sparks their memory.

* Resist the urge to have your child draw a picture to remind them at this point. That can come later when they illustrate their story or idea. <u>They are learning how to depend on letters. Don't take that away from them.</u>
* Sometimes one letter may tell the whole story.

* During these times your child gains confidence in their abilities and in you, and you gain insight into how your child learns. Remember, you aren't there to fix anything and you should never take over the writing. One easy way to do this is simply to be sure you never touch the paper ...with anything. Your physical distance from your child's work displays their ownership of what they write.

* If they ask what a letter looks like, draw it in the air to remind them, point to where it is printed on something else or get your own paper for writing. You are there to help them understand and use what they know. They may need to cross out some letters or add a new one or just find an important letter to remind them of their thought and that will be enough. Respect their process of learning.

* Letter names sound a lot like the sounds each letter makes. Help your writer use the obvious clues as much as possible.

* Basically, just use what works for your child and discover how your child learns independently.

Writing Together

Occasionally, do some writing with your child. Watch how they tackle problems, what comes easily, when frustration starts and when they lose interest. Use what they have learned and how they have learned it in past experiences to help them attach new skills to old. Your examples don't even need to be about writing.

"Remember how you put your blocks pushed up together so your tower wouldn't fall over? You can do that with letters in a word so they can help you remember better."

"Remember when you wrote the letters fast so you didn't worry and add extra letters?"

"Remember when you said the sound you heard in pizza over and over and the letter just popped into your brain?"

"Remember when you learned to spell 'the' because you use it so much? Maybe 'and' is a word that would be nice to remember, too."

"Remember how much you love me?" (Get what you can out of these experiences!)

When you write together make sure your child chooses the topic and dances between reading and writing while they work. As you observe something your child doesn't understand (e.g., remembering what to say, putting sounds together to make words, rereading writing, using periods, using certain sounds, spelling consistently used words) just focus on that one part of the writing experience and help them find success. Do not address multiple needs. Just choose one and let the rest go.

In my kindergarten and first grade classes I called this 'theme editing.' The idea is to encourage them to use a specific skill that will help them be able to write and reread their work better, using their own writing. Keep it short and 'smiley' and maybe they will figure out that they can ask you about homework when they're in the third grade and you won't go 'off' on every little detail. It is really the same idea as talking to children about sex. Just answer what they ask, put your hands in your pockets and don't show your fear.

Whenever you write with your child it should feel like a celebration. You and your child should be having fun. This is the beginning of a tradition of sharing thoughts with each other. Remember, writing is very personal and you are privileged to be included. If it doesn't feel like this to you, don't do it. Sleep on your attitude and try again when you aren't as tired or as pressed for time. Enjoy!

How a writer thinks is as important to learning to write as what a writer does. Think about all the things you automatically do as you write and share your process with your child.

Choosing Topics

First, let your child decide what to write. The first and most important thing a good writer needs is something to say. It can also be one of the hardest things. So.... take your cue from your child.

Start out by just writing what they think is important or funny or happy or sad... Don't create writer's block in a four-year-old by assigning topics or evaluating their ideas. An event, a feeling, a picture or a book might inspire a writer. Just help them find what they want to say. Revising and editing is much easier if you understand and have interest in your topic.

When I taught kindergarten and first grade I had a very influential mentor who was also a professor and well known researcher. One day when visiting my classroom she asked why I wrote on charts (giant pads of paper) with the students. She said that I had words and letters all over the room, why take the time to write on

66

giant pads of paper? (She knew the answer but wanted me to discover it.)

I quit writing on the charts for a few weeks to research the need and it became clear. Although there were models of letters and words all over the room, the process of writing was not specifically dealt with in any other way. Writing together allowed me to display the thinking process of a writer. Understanding this made me write with children, even in one-on-one situations, in a different way. I learned a lot from that experience about the purpose of interactive writing with children.

Developing Independence

Helping children try to control words and sentences reminds me of watching servers in a busy restaurant balance layers of plates and glasses as they move through crowds of jostling diners. You get good at what you do by doing it. A couple of plates for my two hands would be all I could handle unless I also had to walk and not break anything. Encourage your child to take small steps, gather up confidence and play with the power of words.

Remember What You Said?

An independent writer needs to decide what words to use and then hold on to those words as they are written. This step is generally ignored because adults tend to automatically remind children of what comes next as they write. It is actually hard not to remind them.

Often a child's confusion when trying to read their writing reflects the fact that they were confused when they were writing it. As children begin to use more letters, they sometimes lose track of the rest of the sentence as they sound out individual words. Doing this for them just increases dependence. Parents are good at paying attention to their children. So watch them write like you watch them play. You don't play for them. But you do offer occasional advice and support their attempts at new things as you enjoy the show. Help them slow things down once in a while and play with ways to hold on to their words or encourage them to use fewer letters (or worry less) to speed up their writing so they don't get bogged down and forget what they wanted to say. Just see what works best for them.

WRITE and READ, then READ and WRITE,
THEN WRITE and READ.

The most effective way to help your child at every level of writing ability is to consistently allow them to be responsible for reading what they write. Give them lots of chances to read their own writing. Whether it's a grocery list or a story, the experience your child gains develops their ability to look for what they want to say in what they write. This spiraling process of giving themselves better clues for reading what they write, gradually refines their writing. It's a little like hide and seek. The more familiar you are with the area where you are playing the game, the easier it is for you to hide and to find others who are hiding. The little secret places you are familiar with from your past experiences make you a better hider and seeker.

Writing teaches writing.

When you are writing for yourself, read aloud what you write with your child. Reread before you add words or a new sentence. Then encourage your children to read their sentences as they write and reread what they write as they add words. Not only will it help them know what to write next as they write but they will be able to read it more confidently when they finish. "After all that's what grown-ups do."

If the sentences keep changing as they write, they probably need to talk more about what they want to say and focus on writing one thing at a time. Or they may just not be ready to 'hold on to' words yet as they write. If so, talk about what they want to say and let them write a few letters to remind them of the topic.

I Can't Find the Words!

Beginning writers can also gain control of their writing by pointing to the words as they write or read what they have written. Of course you already model this in front of them in many of the things you write or read for them. If they still have a problem finding their words when they read, ask them where just one important word is. Using that single word, you can help them see how to use their writing in a way they can control. It lets them see how even a focus on one word they write can make the whole sentence readable.

In this scenario you help your child write a familiar letter that they can associate with the word in question to help them remember. You can also help them make a sound they hear in the word and match it with a letter. It all depends on what they are ready for. Just keep encouraging them by connecting their writing to what they read.

It's Really Not Like Herding Cats...
Well, Maybe a Little.

Letters can sometimes get overwhelming as children hear more sounds and try to control all the information they end up with. It is really a good sign. But it is also a sign that your child needs a little help working with their writing to regain control. Sometimes children write their words all stuck together in phrases. So they end up with one long word that reads like this, "Aman wassurfingaloneandasharkbithim." But then as children get better at isolating sounds in words, they will often go in the opposite direction and write each syllable or sound unit separately like they are each individual words. Their writing looks like alphabet soup.

All these are normal stages kids can go through as they hold on to their meaning and learn to write it down. But they are impossible to read. When children's writing changes like this it's because they are learning, and trying something new based on that learning. Talk to them. Watch them write and help them understand what they are doing. Sometimes you can just point to the words for them as they read or you might get out your own paper and help them learn about their writing. Copy the letters they wrote on your paper. Then work with their letters to show them what they are doing. Do not use 'correct letters' and show them how to spell the words at this point or you will lose the learning opportunity. Just help them see how to read their own writing by using their letters to form words.

Writing Dependencies

There are little tricks you may occasionally use to help your children gain control of their writing. Be careful that the tools don't turn into dependencies that keep them from developing other skills. Circling, underlining, dashes and even pictures can start off as tools and then limit growth as children depend on the tool rather than the writing. Just watch for the right moment.

If you use tools like these and notice that your children hang on to them, encourage them by saying that they don't need them anymore because they are now better readers or writers. Move through withdrawal together as you show them how to write without tools. On the next page are examples of specifically modeling how to hold on to words or control letter groups etc. while writing.

This is just an outline of a thought process to play with for a short sentence here and there when they are ready. As your child gains experience, motivation and patience you can help them use more skills as they need them to remember and read.

Be careful, when writing together with your child, that you don't overdo it and inadvertently create a dependent, rather than an empowered, writer. Once they understand how to identify words separately, you can modify the same format. But this time, point to spots on the paper to suggest where to write the next word, instead of pointing to fingers. Continue repeating the sentence and writing a new word each time.

Then point to the words your child has just heard five times and help them read it. Vary this as much as you want and enjoy modeling how you write, together. Eventually, everything from sounds to spacing, punctuation, capitalization and spelling can be taught through short experiences of writing together one step at a time.

The common practice of using two fingers to separate words is fine after your child views letter groups as words. If you give them this tool before then, you will have lots of neatly spaced letters that need a passport to get near the other letters in their word. Keep in mind that writing with your child in an instructional way is a tiny part of a bigger picture of literacy in your home.

These ideas are just to help you understand the process so you can help your child with their learning as they write at home. If all you do is help your child use a letter they hear occasionally, they will move along much better than if you push them into tedious writing situations. As you show them letters they hear and ask for, to record signs and stories, they will begin relying on letters to express themselves more and more. Try not to get in the way of your child's explorations. Just be aware of what you do when you depend on writing in daily life in front of your child.

When I started writing with my kindergartners I told them all the things I could write about like
     -brushing my teeth and how the toothpaste escaped my mouth sometimes and how weird it is to spit,
     -OR driving to school with my clean car and driving through a puddle and knowing there would be splashes on my car,
     -OR. OR, OR...
I would just bore them with my life full of meaningless events. Then I would explain that when you don't know what to write it is never because you don't have anything to say. It is always because you have too much to say and you can't decide. "It's like all the ideas are crowded and squished up at the door and none of them can get out. So I just pick one and write and stop worrying." This attitude gave my students confidence and a positive slant on choosing topics.

Even the university students I taught displayed the importance of topic in writing. The students who reviewed articles they didn't really understand wrote poorly. I could barely even decipher what they were trying to say. But when the same students wrote about articles they comprehended well, their writing totally changed. Even at the college level, the more we know and enjoy our topics the better we write about them.

A kindergartner I had in class wrote the card on the following page for his mom on mother's day. He was thanking his mom for teaching him how to walk by remembering her process.

Use the samples on these 3 pages to hone your skills as a word sleuth. It's a bit like charades with no rules

.

But it's a helpful beginning for communication and empowerment at home. Peaking at 'translations' might be a rule infraction.

1

Powr ☯weN feet FoD AnD
an P in The eh Down

2

1at me Com You o ɗAn

You are got it

4

Tou Ce Cep Doine A
Y oV 9ot +i

5

☯ You CoLD Dot i NoV

6

Van You Momy

Translation: <u>"Put one foot down and one foot up in the air. Let me show you again. You are getting it. You got it! You can do it now. Thank you, mom."</u>

Writing samples: page one

A man was
surfing alone and
a shark bit him.>>

Wat I WONT
To Bee

I WONT To Bee
a ZKOOBa Diveer
Theez are zom
Of The Thingz I
am going To use;

<< <u>What I Want to Be</u>
I want to be a scuba diver.
These are some of the
things I am going to use.

<u>The picture below</u> shows a
child using art and writing to
get his point across.

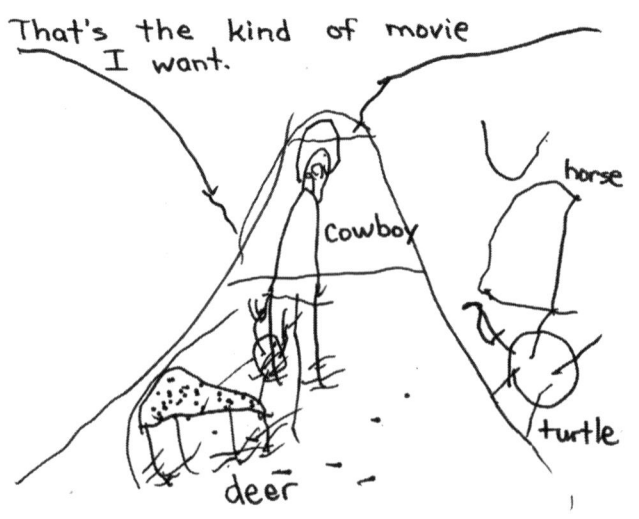

That's the kind of movie
I want.

horse

Cowboy

turtle

deer

Writing samples: page two

The chickens hatched! black and white, 2 inches, cute.

Translation: I really miss you when you are in choir.

Translation: Dear Mommy, This picture was from my wall. These letters are gonna be smaller. Josh is working on his book. Before he mails his letter why don't you please make me a letter right now. The magic word is 'please'.

I Love You Mommy.

Writing samples: page three

YOU WRITE

A metaphor of learning to write
Written By: A Kindergarten Boy

1. Some things are too hard for me.

2. Writing is too hard

3. When you are going along you run into hard sounds.

4. Sometimes you run into rocks.

5. When you run into hard parts you run Into nails

6. Writing is Totally fun For me..

7. You have to stop and get quieter.

8. You put down the letter you hear.

9. Writing is So easy for me

10. You see so Much stuff When you write. .

11. When you ride in the car you don't worry about nails and rocks..

12 You look out the window.

13 You see trees, houses, restaurants and people.

14. But you don't worry..

READING,
THE BEST FRIEND OF WRITING

"Outside of a dog, a book is a man's best friend.
Inside of a dog, it's too hard to read."
- Groucho Marx

There are already lots of books about reading to children but I can't really talk about writing without involving reading. I have included some general thoughts and a few specific suggestions about reading at different stages with children. Learning to be independent with books and how to explore and talk about books is an important part of learning to be a writer.

The experiences you provide, the attitude you model and the atmosphere you create with books will influence your child's learning well beyond the printed pages. Ask your favorite reader, librarian or friend. There are new book ideas everywhere and classics that again gain respect with a new generation.

Often a series is nice because your child gains history and comfort as a new author is explored. As children become more social, books and authors enter topics of group conversations on the playground and fodder for phone conversations that normally start out as blank air time.

Babies and Toddlers

Chewable books (cardboard, rubber, plastic, material) are the books of choice for babies and toddlers. Books with only pictures, a few words, songs or repetitive language are very appropriate and easy for parents to share while they encourage their book eaters to

appreciate words and stories that leave a memorable taste for books in their amazing brain. Leave these books out and use them like toys while babies and toddlers get comfortable with them and start bringing them to adults to secure lap space and a time of adult attention and touch using a book. When you use books with babies and toddlers, have no expectations. Enjoy the cuddle. Even a busy day can stop for a book.

Actually, you know it will be a short stop (no baseball metaphor intended) because attention span is measured in seconds at this age. Enjoy the moment. Don't insist on finishing the book, unless you are really caught up in the plot in which case an outing to the public library may be in order for mommy or daddy. If you pay attention you will start to see the little reader emerge in these early experiences. These may seem like little things. But by understanding and celebrating them, your child learns to look at books with more confidence and is encouraged to investigate. You will be able to enjoy lots of small things that show you your child is learning, if you just watch.

Preschoolers and Kindergarteners

Books with paper pages are better to bring out after children begin enjoying stories without having to love the books to death. Favorite books are important to read over and over. They become metaphors used in daily experiences and are discussed during family meals. Shared books become uniting experiences, almost like vacations. Everyone has had the same experience, even if each one gets something different out of it. The trick is to learn to appreciate the 'something different' each person brings to the discussion. When that happens, books and people connect. Readers gain perspective in what they read and learn to appreciate the opinions of others.

Fairy Tales, Nursery Rhymes and Classics

"If you want your children to be intelligent, read them fairy tales. If you want them to be more intelligent, read them more fairy tales." -Albert Einstein

Fairytales, nursery rhymes and childhood classics are important literature for any reader. Metaphors from children's books are often used in other literature, as well as in movies and everyday conversation. Understanding those metaphors . can make a big difference in becoming literate in many areas.

Fun With Words

"The boy who cried, 'Wolf." "Sour grapes." "I feel like Cinderella." "You're feeling a bit like Alice. Hmm? Tumbling down the rabbit hole?" "We're off to see the wizard." "Not by the hair of my chinny, chin, chin." "A trail of bread crumbs." "Your nose is growing." And my personal favorite, "Grandma, what big teeth you have!"

Word fun books are especially grand for 3-4 year olds. Books with multi-syllable words, and character names, rhyming words and silly phrases, encourage play with words and draw attention to the sounds of words, syllabication and the flow and flexibility of language. Mercer Mayer and Dr. Seuss are especially good authors for word play.

Repetition, All Over Again

As your child wants to become more independent in their reading, books with repetitive or predictable phrasing and songs and poems come into fashion and enhance confidence. Then motivation takes over and children read and reread favorites. This familiarity with books allows your child to take risks by reading along and then experimenting with other kinds of books. Eventually, this creates interest in all the print that stamps their world (names of stores and products, words on signs, etc.), which now means you need to avoid those grocery store check-out stands displaying lurid tabloids.

Support Reading at Home

A home library doesn't have to be expensive. Garage sales, used bookstores, second hand shops and friends are excellent sources for books. Also, putting books at the top of birthday and Christmas wish lists sends an important message. Frequent visits to the library will help you multiply your book experiences without having to build more shelves. The public library is your best source of expertise and resources in this area.

You are a critical part of your child's reading that goes beyond just buying books and reading aloud. You need to model being a reader yourself. Watching parents spending time reading and enjoying their own books, is a big motivator for young readers. Of course, if you are the type that gets so engrossed that you need someone to wrench the book from your hand in order to stop and feed your children, pace yourself! Set a time each day to relax and read. Read aloud at first and then plan a few minutes for all family members to spend time alone with books. This time will move from 5 minutes to 20 or more as your child matures and becomes more confident and focused on individual book interaction.

These experiences are most successful when everyone takes a break and reads. Sometimes parents get so caught up with the business of living, they lose touch with even having an idea of something they want to read beyond incoming mail. If that is the case, go to the public library and get ideas from a librarian. They are excellent resources. As parents of young children, a short vacation in a book is a welcome 'outing' that doesn't require a babysitter. In my own kindergarten classes, the minute I began to say it was time to stop reading during independent reading time, the groans and begging for a few more minutes would start. It is glorious to watch a child engrossed in reading.

Reading Stories to Children

1: Pick books your child enjoys.
Try to find books your child requests or books that fit with something current in your child's life. For example, weather related stories, books about animals they have seen or played with, event books (sickness, parades, holidays, new babies, etc.), or, most importantly, books that help you laugh together.
You don't want to sit through a short advertisement, much less a movie, about something you have no interest in. And there is no way you would keep reading a book if it didn't hold your interest. So keep that in mind as you choose books for your child. Early on, funny voices alone can make most any book interesting to a little one, but later children make their preferences very clear.

Also, understand that when a child likes a book, you may be reading it often and with many readings per sitting. These multiple readings are actually very important. As children become familiar with a book they find more to look at. They also begin to pay more attention to words and patterns of language, like rhyming or easily predictable phrases (e.g., Brown Bear, Brown Bear, by Bill Martin). Soon they begin to play with the words used in books as much as the pictures. These repeated stories may also be the first ones your child chooses to read on his or her own.

2: Interrupted stories are hard to follow.

When I read, I don't like being interrupted. If I don't understand something, I have learned to make sense of it in context and go back later if it affects how I understand the story, or I just want to learn more about whatever it was. Learning to make sense of a text in context, creates independence. An easy way to help

I learned the importance of this from one of my kindergarten classes. I used to read books and stop to comment while I read. The children also made comments, had conversations and played with the carpet and their Velcro shoes. One distraction-ridden day, my class started a discussion about interrupting stories. A little boy told the class that when people interrupt a story it is like he is on a field trip and someone just grabs him 'right off the bus.' The next day, after further discussion before a new book, the class made a rule that no one could interrupt a story until the reading was finished. That included the verbose teacher. We also decided that we would read books twice if we needed to talk about them. What happened was amazing. Everyone listened and the comments afterward were at a different level. When we read through the second time the children asked questions, I asked questions, sometimes we had answers, but everyone enjoyed the story in their own way.

children develop this approach to reading is to let them form their own opinions and understanding by listening to the author as you read the book without interruptions.

Then, once the reading is done, reread and investigate, stop and start, go back and forth in the book and interrupt all you want. Reading a book, forming your own opinions, listening to the thoughts of others and looking again at the book in a new way is what literature study is all about. I am not talking about book clubs or school groups here. I am talking about studying literature by reading, paying attention, forming opinions, making your own sense out of what you read and discussing it with others.

Sharing a book with a friend, learning about what others notice and articulating your own thoughts with others connects us and takes us to unexplored places.

Behaving like a reader can create a reader. Reading expands our knowledge base and gives us a chance to see life through another person's eyes.

3: Story interaction is important.

Mem Fox, the author of many children's books, said, "Writing a picture book is like writing <u>War and Peace</u> in Haiku." Picture books have a lot to offer. As an adult reader, you share with your child more than just words read aloud. A computerized book could do that. You expand the meaning of each book you read just by sitting with your child. The closeness of sharing a book page affects the experience of reading. But there's more. Your honest comments, questions and possible references to the book in future books or experiences, make books and reading personal.

This creates a connection to literature that builds confidence in your children. Lifelong readers are able to connect to the books they read. They can see and talk about the places books take them. Often people are disappointed with movies based on books they have read. The imagination of the reader usually surpasses the skill level of the filmmaker and the interpretation of each is likely to differ. In other words ... no worries. Whatever you suppose, as the reader, is important and should be explored.

As your child gets older and more skilled at discussion, use the book to back up opinions. This will add depth and more honesty to book discussions. As you talk about a book, try to turn to the pages being discussed as you talk. This acknowledges individual comments and may spark more conversation about your child's ideas. An additional benefit is that when you take the time to turn to the page they are discussing you are respecting their comment, physically. Often that is all that is needed.

The children in my kindergarten/first grade classes expected each other to explain their thoughts using the book. The first thing they did when making a comment was to turn to the page or ask me to turn to the page to show it to the class when they said something. This started simply as I quietly turned to the page they were talking about and displayed it.

React
Just stating what you noticed in the book is a good start. Then listen to what your child says or does and

affirm their ideas. It doesn't need to be profound. Simple is good. Try not to evaluate, just react to the book. If you or your child does give an evaluation, follow up with an explanation.

Respond

As you talk about books with your child, the words you use in response to comments are also important. Responses that sound like evaluations take the power away from your child and give it to you. (e.g., "Right!" "That's good." "You're so smart.") Respond to your child's comments with your take on the issue or acknowledge their comment by adding to it.

"Right!" may become, "I didn't notice that." "That's good," might be, "Show me where you saw that." And, "You're so smart," could change to, "How did you think of that?"

Pay Attention

Sometimes, ideas that children present when talking about books may seem incorrect. First, remember that this is a discussion and opinions are just opinions. But often when you dig deeper into what a child says that may seem "off", you find a metaphor lurking behind it. For example, if your child is talking about the dog page in Brown Bear, Brown Bear What Do You See? by Bill Martin, and says, "My head was hurting," and starts to cry, you may find that what he is really saying is he misses his friend who moved away. (The picture reminded your child of his friend's dog that pushed him down one day and made him bump his head.) Maybe that is the discussion you need to have and put the book aside for later. A book is often a vehicle for other discussions. You can learn a lot by reading, listening and asking questions. Talking about books can help you understand your child and create respectful habits for future conversations.

Metaphors or Misinformation?
"You do not really understand something unless you can explain it to your grandmother."
-Albert Einstein

Asking about your child's thinking process lets your child know you value his/her opinions. I don't know what Einstein had against grandmothers, but the truth is you really DO understand something if you can explain it to a five-year-old.

Play with your children. Talk to them. Surround them with opportunities to expand their learning. Give them time to sit and reflect and most importantly listen to them. Writing provides the opportunity for, and at the same time requires, all of the above.

The kids who didn't listen in class were shocked when I asked them about something they said. They weren't used to their words having importance and therefore had no respect for the words of others.

Stopping what we are doing and listening to a child is a significantly effective parenting and teaching skill. There may be an important metaphor or a bit of misinformation ready to be unwrapped inside a seemingly bizarre comment. Remember, reading, writing and talking are all interdependent. So encourage communication.

It's Like...

A few years ago, my son told me he had just taken his three-year-old daughter to bed for the second time that night and, in his words, "...a little while later she came back in, this time quoting the Grinch story, 'Why, Santy Claus? Why are you taking our Christmas tree? Why?' in her best quiet, adorable, Cindy Lu Who voice." Of course he couldn't send her back to bed.

......teaching your child to ride a bike. You run alongside until they are ready to take off on their own. Don't get worn out from too much running. Relax and make sure you both

enjoy the ride. Write with your child, watch them grow and have fun in the process. Riders, just like swimmers, are taught how to ride or swim, but they don't really go anywhere interesting while someone else is holding them up. They need to be aware of the whole process to use the bike effectively. Then... independence brings along learning and confidence and purpose. They are no longer inhibited by fear of mistakes, and now begin to explore and learn!

Translation:
How to ride a bike.
You have to go fast so
you can ride a two
wheeler. And if you are
going right you turn left.

HAU to rid Aaic
u HArtO GO FAST
SAO U CAN rid AS
cY Lr Aa iF Yr GoYN
riT u TrN LAFT

PRESCHOOL & DAY CARE:
EXTENDING THE EXPERIENCE

"The secret of education lies in respecting the pupil."
Ralph Waldo Emerson

The writing ideas mentioned in this book are also effective in preschool, kindergarten & daycare. Use writing as an integrated part of the day rather than just gluing popcorn on the letter "P".

Support your teachers' own ideas about how to infuse their day with writing.

* Donate recycled paper from your home or business.

* Volunteer to come in once a week for an hour and take dictation from kids about their artwork or just let them"read" their squiggles to you. Volunteer to come in and read with small groups or individual children.

* If your preschool can't leave things on walls because of shared space issues, take pictures and labels home and put them in clear sleeves and notebooks to create books children can look at and recognize their contributions at school.

* Anything you do to help your preschool helps your children and their friends. Get involved. Volunteering also helps hone your skills as a parent and a person.

* Starbucks is welcome anywhere!

KNOW YOUR CHILD

"Do not train a child to learn by force or harshness, just be consistent even when it's hard but direct them to it by what amuses their minds, so that you may be better able to discover with accuracy the peculiar bent of the genius of each." -Plato

You are the best advocate for your child and for his/her teacher. Take some time before school starts and observe your child. Actually, take some notes as you think on what you know about your child. Let your teacher know what encourages a good mood and calms an 'attitude'. Triggers, fears, gifts and allergies are all important. Understand even with all the information you can give the teacher, you both are going to need each other. Through the year, things you share will come to mind that will help the teacher, plan, and your child learn more effectively. Watch your child grow. Use this time well and have fun!

All Children are Gifted

We all are guilty of wanting our children to excel and pushing a little too hard once in a while. We also worry that our child isn't going to do well. But our focus should be on wanting them to excel in life, not just the first grade. We really want them to love reading and write to us when they move out to go to college or find a job that appreciates who he/she is.

Everyone has brilliant and bizarre stories of children exploring and learning. Cherish those glimpses into a beautiful, innocent world. Surround those moments with confident, appropriate expectations. But never judge. Just listen, encourage and see different sides of your darling. School is a whole new world that inspires and grows everyone concerned.
I made it my mission, when I was teaching, to find the gifts in the children I taught...keep your eyes open!

Info for Interpreters

READING WORDS WITHIN SEEMINGLY RANDOM LETTERS

Here is a simple demo chart that may help you organize those crazy letters by grouping them. The more new writers use their writing, the faster they will use letters more effectively and become confident.

Remember: Communication is more important than spelling unless the young writers are interviewing for jobs?

If the letters are stuck in phrases: Maybe circle the words in the group of letters.
"IWNT2O2ASRNBIHUS" might become,
"(I) (WNT) 2 (O) 2 (A) (SR) (N) (BI) (HUS)"

Then read aloud, "I want to go to a store and buy shoes." Point to each word as you read. You don't want them to get into a habit of circling words but it may help them see what they are doing occasionally. Just don't let it become a crutch.*

If the letters are divided by syllables or sound units: Maybe circle the syllables into words.
"M   I   M   O   M   E   E   Z   M   FR   E   BS FND   SH   LFS   E." might become,
" (MI) (MOME) (EZ) (M) (FRE) (BS) (FND). (SH) (LFS) (E)."

Then read aloud, "My mommy is my very best friend. She loves me." Point to each word as you read.

GATHERING WORDS INTO SENTENCES

This example is more detailed than you need. Just help your child identify letter groups and see how they work together to make words. They can circle the letters together for some of the words. just don't let circling get in the way. You will know when your child doesn't need it.

Child: _"The butterfly is yellow."_

Parent: _"Did you say, 'The butterfly is yellow? It certainly is a yellow butterfly."_

Parent and/or Child: _"Let's count the words for, 'The butterfly is yellow. You repeat the sentence with them._

"The - butterfly - is - yellow."

Parent and/or Child: _Count the fingers used._   _(At this point you could stop and say, "What was your favorite word?"   Then point to the finger you used for that word and encourage your child to write any letter/s for any sound/s they hear in that word.   Then ignore the rest of this dialogue and enjoy drawing butterflies.   Keep it positive and short.) OR move on._

Parent: _"What was this word?" Point to the first finger you   used in the sentence._

Parent and/or Child: _"The"_

Parent: _Write 'The.'   Read, 'The'_

Parent: _"Let's say it again, 'The – butterfly – is – yellow."_

Each time, use your fingers as you say the sentence and point to the finger for the next word. You might start the sentence and stop on the word that comes next and let them remember it on their own. Keep repeating this general format encouraging your child to give you the word or saying it with them.

A Visit With an Author

Writing can be emotional and powerful, no matter the age or experience of the writer or the reader (our kindergarten class). We previously read one of this author's books, and cried our way through the ending earlier that year. Since he was only going to be with our class for a short time, the class decided on a student's book for the author to read to them. They chose a book one of the students had recently written. The book left everyone teary eyed, including our visitor.

Here is the text of the book

Nana and Mom.

By: A Kindergartener

One night we called Nana. She did
not answer. My dad guessed she was on her
machine. We called again at nine o'clock. She still
did not answer. My mom was getting worried. My
dad went over. My dad found her lying in bed. My
dad came home to tell my mom she was dead. We
went to church the next day. After church we went
home. We were sad. When my mom went to school
the next day, at break time my mom went to the
library. Lots of friends were there. They gave her
flowers. When my dad and mom picked me up I saw
lots of flowers in the van. In a few days my mom's
brothers came over. It was getting dark. Then my
cousins came over from the airport. We had fun.
But we miss our Nana. My Nana couldn't breathe all
my mom's life. My mom is happy about one thing.
My Nana can breathe well now...because she is in
heaven.

---

*As the author finished reading the kindergartner's book
he looked at me with tears in his eyes and said, "You
did this on purpose." He was right. After he left the
room, my students couldn't stop talking about how one
of their books made a famous author cry. They learned
their writing could affect others. Some of the things
your children write will make you laugh or cry. Be
careful that you don't step on their writing in the name
of teaching.*

ABOUT THE AUTHOR

By: Carole Edelsky
Ph.D., Professor Emerita, Arizona State
University

Chris Rathkey taught primary age children in Phoenix for 35 years. She has a master's degree from the University of Arizona and has won several awards for outstanding teaching. She taught teachers at Arizona State University and in numerous other cities by means of her videotaped teaching shown at professional development sessions. How lucky you are to be able to learn from Chris Rathkey's brilliant, innovative yet imminently sensible, well-grounded advice!

It's been almost four decades since I first saw Chris Rathkey (then Chris Boyd) teaching; almost four decades since I introduced my teacher preparation students to her kindergarten classroom to see what truly extraordinary teaching looks like. I've videotaped her teaching and used these videos so master teachers around North America could learn from them.

I've seen researchers and university professors from around the world visit her classroom to learn from how she taught very young learners. And today, I get to do what she does not do—act as her press agent, because, as my grandmother used to say, "she doesn't toot her own horn."

Chris Rathkey's ability to turn children on to literacy is legendary. Year after year, her kindergarten students grew by leaps and bounds as writers. How did she do that? By doing what she writes about in this book (If Only the Bears Had Left a Note). She refuses to underestimate children or to overwhelm them or to short circuit their independence. She combines her deep understanding of literacy with her keen sense of practicality. She respects children's thinking and knows how to lead them to think more deeply. She inspires them, through very deliberate ways of speaking that she describes in this book, to grow as thinkers and writers. The result is that, with purpose and intention, she brings written language along into daily life as she loves, plays with, and guides children.

Create memories.
Appreciate laughter.
Enjoy your children.

Teach a child in a way that fits their needs and even when they are old they will not leave the right path.- Proverbs 22:6

Remember, your children will be in charge of your grandchildren.

i KANRib m iBig
BiC i FXLGAb

Translation: I can ride my big bike. I feel good.

Literacy Events

Literacy Events

Notes